WITHDRAWN

States

NORTH CAROLINA

by Tyler Maine

CAPSTONE PRESS
a capstone imprint

Next Page Books are published by Capstone Press,
1710 Roe Crest Drive, North Mankato, Minnesota 56003
www.mycapstone.com

Library of Congress Cataloging-in-Publication Data
Cataloging-in-publication information is on file with the Library of
Congress.
ISBN 978-1-5157-0420-1 (library binding)
ISBN 978-1-5157-0479-9 (paperback)
ISBN 978-1-5157-0531-4 (ebook PDF)

Editorial Credits
Jaclyn Jaycox, editor; Kazuko Collins and Katy LaVigne, designers;
Morgan Walters, media researcher; Tori Abraham, production specialist

Photo Credits
Capstone Press: Angi Gahler, map 4, 7; CriaImages.com: Jay Robert
Nash Collection, bottom 18, bottom 19; Dreamstime: Jerry Coli, top 18,
photographer, top right 21; Getty Images: Hulton Fine Art Collection/
The British Library/Robana, top 19; Library of Congress: Prints
and Photographs Division Washington, D.C., 27, 28, Jesse Harrison
Whitehurst, middle 18; Newscom: Picture History, 26; North Wind
Picture Archives, 12, 25; One Mile Up, Inc., flag, seal 23; Shutterstock:
Action Sports Photography, bottom 24, bluebullet, top right 20,
Boykung, top left 21, Connie Barr, bottom left 20, Daniel Prudek,
bottom left 21, digidreamgrafix, 5, bottom left 8, Erni, middle right 21,
IrinaK, bottom right 20, Jason Grindle, 13, Jason Patrick Ross, middle
left 21, jdwfoto, 9, John Wollwerth, 16, Jorg Hackemann, 10, Joseph
Sohm, 11, karenfoleyphotography, 17, Local Favorite Photography,
14, Looker_Studio, top 24, MarkVanDykePhotography, cover, 6, Mary
Terriberry, 15, Paul Orr, bottom right 21, s_bukley, middle 19, Serge
Skiba, bottom right 8, SergeyIT, top left 20, traxlergirl, 7; Wikimedia:
U.S. Fish and Wildlife Service Southeast Region, 29

All design elements by Shutterstock

Printed and bound in China.
0316/CA21600187
012016 009436F16

TABLE OF CONTENTS

Want to take your research further? Ask your librarian if your school subscribes to PebbleGo Next. If so, when you see this helpful symbol (↖) throughout the book, log onto www.pebblegonext.com for bonus downloads and information.

LOCATION

North Carolina is located in the southeastern United States. The Atlantic Ocean borders North Carolina to the east. The state is bordered by Virginia on the north and Tennessee on the west. Georgia and South Carolina lie to the south. North Carolina's capital is Raleigh, which is one of the state's largest cities. North Carolina's other large cities include Charlotte, Greensboro, Winston-Salem, and Durham.

PebbleGo Next Bonus!
To print and label
your own map, go to
www.pebblegonext.com
and search keywords:

NC MAP

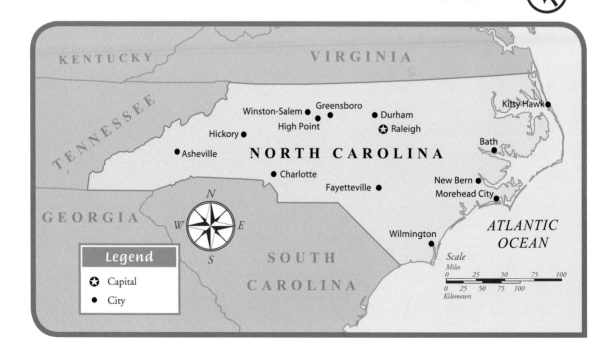

KENTUCKY

VIRGINIA

TENNESSEE

Kitty Hawk●

Winston-Salem ● ●Greensboro
●High Point ● Durham
Hickory ● ✪ Raleigh

NORTH CAROLINA

Bath ●

● Asheville

● Charlotte

Fayetteville ●

New Bern ●
Morehead City ●

GEORGIA

N
W ● *E*
S

SOUTH

CAROLINA

Wilmington ●

ATLANTIC
OCEAN

Scale
Miles
0   25   50   75   100

0   25   50   75   100
Kilometers

Legend

✪   Capital

●   City

Nicknamed the Queen City, Charlotte is North Carolina's largest city.

GEOGRAPHY

North Carolina is divided into the Atlantic Coastal Plain, the Piedmont, and the Mountain Region. The Coastal Plain covers eastern North Carolina. The plain spreads inland from the coast. The Piedmont is a hilly region with many rivers and the state's biggest cities. The Mountain Region forms a border between North Carolina, Georgia, and Tennessee. North Carolina's Mount Mitchell rises 6,684 feet (2,037 meters) above sea level. It is the highest peak in eastern North America.

PebbleGo Next Bonus!
To watch a video about Cape Lookout National Seashore, go to www.pebblegonext.com and search keywords:

NC VIDEO

The Appalachian Trail on the western border of North Carolina offers a view of the Blue Ridge Mountains.

The Outer Banks is a long chain of islands stretching from Virginia to South Carolina. The islands separate North Carolina from the Atlantic Ocean.

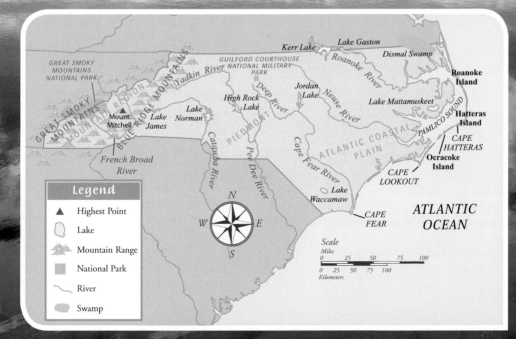

Legend

▲ Highest Point

Lake

Mountain Range

National Park

River

Swamp

GREAT SMOKY MOUNTAINS NATIONAL PARK

GREAT SMOKY MOUNTAINS

BLUE RIDGE MOUNTAINS

MOUNTAIN REGION

Mount Mitchell

French Broad River

Lake James

Lake Norman

Catawba River

PIEDMONT

Yadkin River

GUILFORD COURTHOUSE NATIONAL MILITARY PARK

High Rock Lake

Deep River

Jordan Lake

Kerr Lake

Lake Gaston

Roanoke River

Dismal Swamp

Neuse River

Lake Mattamuskeet

ATLANTIC COASTAL PLAIN

Pee Dee River

Cape Fear River

Lake Waccamaw

CAPE FEAR

CAPE LOOKOUT

Ocracoke Island

PAMLICO SOUND

Roanoke Island

Hatteras Island

CAPE HATTERAS

ATLANTIC OCEAN

N W E S

Scale
Miles
0   25   50   75   100
0 25 50 75 100
Kilometers

WEATHER

North Carolina's climate varies with the region. The Atlantic Coastal Plain and the Piedmont have warmer summers and winters than the Mountain Region. The average January temperature in North Carolina is 41 degrees Fahrenheit (5 degrees Celsius). The average July temperature is 70°F (21°C).

Average High and Low Temperatures (Charlotte, NC)

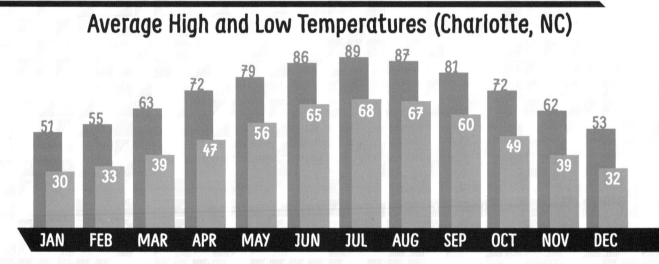

	JAN	FEB	MAR	APR	MAY	JUN	JUL	AUG	SEP	OCT	NOV	DEC
High	51	55	63	72	79	86	89	87	81	72	62	53
Low	30	33	39	47	56	65	68	67	60	49	39	32

Mount Mitchell

North Carolina's Mount Mitchell is more than a mile high. At 6,684 feet (2,037 m), Mount Mitchell is the highest point east of the Mississippi River.

Cape Hatteras

Cape Hatteras has America's tallest lighthouse. It was moved to a new location in 1999 because beach erosion threatened to topple it.

Fontana Dam

Fontana Dam near Bryson City is
the tallest concrete dam in the eastern
United States. It is 480 feet (146 m) tall.

HISTORY AND GOVERNMENT

An early American Indian village in North Carolina

American Indians were the earliest residents of North Carolina. They included the Cherokee and Tuscarora people. In the 1500s people from England began moving in. Settlers came from Virginia around 1653 to form a colony. In 1712 Carolina split into North and South Carolina. In time, the colonists wanted freedom from Great Britain. They fought the British in the Revolutionary War (1775–1783). In 1783 the colonists won the war and became free from Great Britain. North Carolina became the 12th state in 1789.

North Carolina's state government has three branches. The legislature makes laws for the state. It consists of the Senate with 50 members and the House of Representatives with 120 members. As the leader of the executive branch, the governor signs bills into law. Judges make up the judicial branch. They uphold the laws.

The exterior walls of the capitol building are made of gneiss. The rock was quarried from Raleigh and brought down by the state's first railway.

INDUSTRY

Agriculture has been a major part of North Carolina's economy since colonial times. The state is a top producer of turkeys, chickens, and hogs. North Carolina also leads the nation in tobacco production.

North Carolina ranks second in the nation for turkey production.

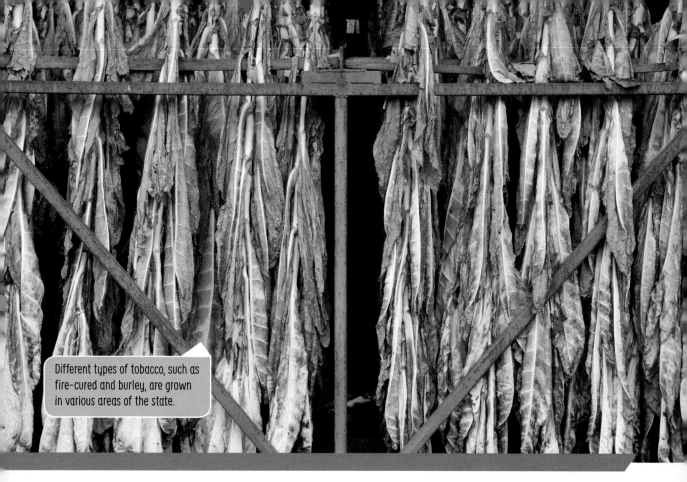

Different types of tobacco, such as fire-cured and burley, are grown in various areas of the state.

While farmland covers about one-third of the state, manufacturing and service industries produce more income for North Carolina than farming does. North Carolina produces medicines, cleaning products, fertilizers, tobacco products, textiles, furniture, and rubber products. Education, health care, research, retail, and other service industries are a major part of the state's economy. Tourism and banking are among its largest service industries.

POPULATION

Many North Carolinians are descendants of the state's first European settlers. The state has one of the largest Scots-Irish populations in the United States. Other North Carolinians have English or German backgrounds.

Other ethnicities are represented in North Carolina. African-Americans are North Carolina's second-largest ethnic group. They compose about 20 percent of the state's population. Hispanics are about 8 percent of the state's population. American Indians make up 1 percent of the population, and Asian Americans are less than 3 percent of North Carolina's population.

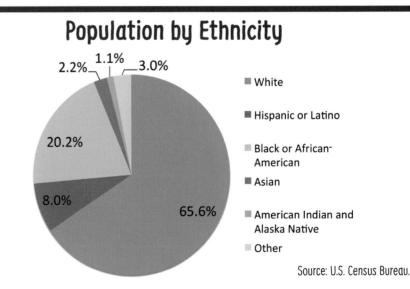

Population by Ethnicity

- 2.2%
- 1.1%
- 3.0%
- 20.2%
- 8.0%
- 65.6%

- White
- Hispanic or Latino
- Black or African-American
- Asian
- American Indian and Alaska Native
- Other

Source: U.S. Census Bureau.

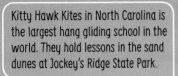

Kitty Hawk Kites in North Carolina is the largest hang gliding school in the world. They hold lessons in the sand dunes at Jockey's Ridge State Park.

FAMOUS PEOPLE

Michael Jordan (1963–) is called the world's greatest basketball player. He played for the UNC Tar Heels before joining the National Basketball Association (NBA).

Andrew Johnson (1808–1875) was the 17th president of the United States (1865–1869). He was born in Raleigh.

James Polk (1795–1849) was the 11th president of the United States (1845–1849). He was born in Mecklenburg County.

Levi Coffin (1798–1877) was a leader in the Underground Railroad in Indiana. This system helped slaves escape to freedom. He was born in Greensboro.

Dale Earnhardt Jr. (1974–) is a championship-winning NASCAR driver and the son of NASCAR racer Dale Earnhardt Sr. He was born in Kannapolis.

William Sydney Porter (1862–1910) wrote many short stories. He used the pen name O. Henry. He was born in Greensboro.

STATE SYMBOLS

Tree

pine

Flower

dogwood

Bird

cardinal

Fish

channel bass

PebbleGo Next Bonus! To make a popular North Carolina dessert, go to www.pebblegonext.com and search keywords:

NC RECIPE

Gemstone

emerald

Fruit

Scuppernong grape

Reptile

eastern box turtle

Animal

gray squirrel

Insect

honeybee

Shell

scotch bonnet

FAST FACTS

STATEHOOD
1789

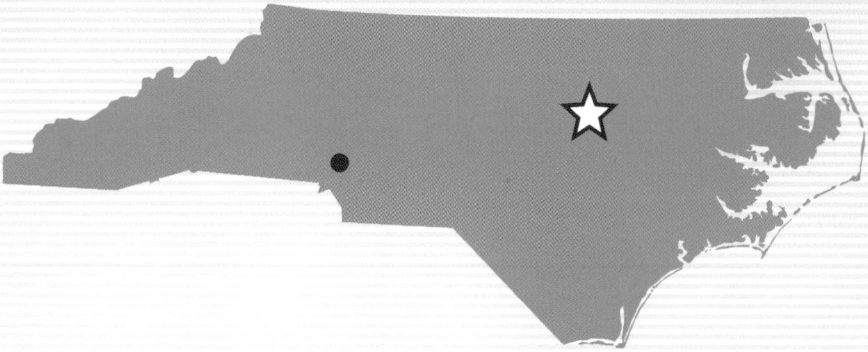

CAPITAL ☆
Raleigh

LARGEST CITY ●
Charlotte

SIZE
48,618 square miles (125,920 square kilometers) land area
(2010 U.S. Census Bureau)

POPULATION
9,848,060 (2013 U.S. Census estimate)

STATE NICKNAME
Tar Heel State

STATE MOTTO
"Esse Quam Videri," which is Latin for "to be rather than to seem"

STATE SEAL

The state seal of North Carolina shows the goddesses Liberty and Plenty. Liberty stands for freedom. Plenty represents agriculture. Two dates from the state flag are also on the seal. In the background are mountains and a ship. They stand for the state's land and trade. The state motto, "Esse Quam Videri," is at the bottom.

PebbleGo Next Bonus! To print and color your own flag, go to www.pebblegonext.com and search keywords:

NC FLAG

STATE FLAG

North Carolina adopted its flag in 1885. The flag's right side is red on the top and white on the bottom. The left side is dark blue with a white star separating the letters N and C. A ribbon above the star shows the date of the Mecklenberg Declaration of Independence, which is believed to have been signed on May 20, 1775, to declare independence from Great Britain. A ribbon beneath the star has the date of the Halifax Resolves, which allowed North Carolina's leaders to vote for independence from Great Britain.

MINING PRODUCTS

granite, limestone, traprock

MANUFACTURED GOODS

chemicals, food products, computer and electronic equipment, machinery, plastics, electrical equipment, clothing

FARM PRODUCTS

hogs, chickens, decorative plants, tobacco, soybeans

PROFESSIONAL SPORTS TEAMS

Charlotte Hornets (NBA)
Carolina Panthers (NFL)
Carolina Hurricanes (NHL)
Charlotte Sting (WNBA)

PebbleGo Next Bonus!
To learn the lyrics to
the state song, go to
www.pebblegonext.com
and search keywords:
NC SONG

NORTH CAROLINA TIMELINE

1524 About 35,000 American Indians are living in North Carolina when Italian Giovanni da Verrazano explores the mouth of the Cape Fear River.

1585 The English build a colony on Roanoke Island off the coast of present-day North Carolina.

1590 John White finds Roanoke Colony deserted.

1620 The Pilgrims establish a colony in the New World in present-day Massachusetts.

 **1705** People settle near the Pamlico River in a settlement that becomes Bath, North Carolina's first town.

 **1775–1783** American colonists and the British fight the Revolutionary War.

 **1789** North Carolina becomes the 12th state.

 1838 More than 15,000 Cherokee in North Carolina and other eastern states are forced to leave their homeland. They travel to present-day Oklahoma. Thousands of American Indians die during the journey, known as the Trail of Tears.

1861–1865 The Union and the Confederacy fight the Civil War. North Carolina fights on the side of the Confederacy.

1868 North Carolina rejoins the United States of America.

1903 The Wright brothers make the first successful powered airplane flight at Kitty Hawk.

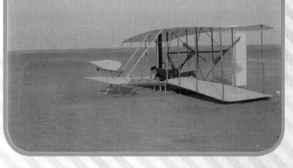

1914–1918 World War I is fought; the United States enters the war in 1917.

1918 Camp Bragg opens near Fayetteville. It later becomes Fort Bragg.

1929–1939 The United States experiences the Great Depression.

1939–1945 World War II is fought; the United States enters the war in 1941.

1960 Four African-Americans hold a sit-in after they are refused service at a lunch counter in Greensboro.

1964 U.S. Congress passes the Civil Rights Act, which makes any form of discrimination illegal.

1989 North Carolinians celebrate their state's 200th birthday.

1999 Hurricane Floyd strikes North Carolina on September 16, killing more than 50 people in the state and causing $6 billion in damage.

2011 Hurricane Irene hits North Carolina on August 20. The hurricane causes more than $7 billion in damage. Millions of homes and businesses lose power.

2015 Scientists at Duke University grow human skeletal muscle for the first time in history.

Glossary

descend *(dee-SEND)*—if you are descended from someone, you belong to a later generation of the same family

discriminate *(dis-KRI-muh-nayt)*—to treat people unfairly because of their skin color or class

erosion *(i-ROH-zhuhn)*—the wearing away of land by water or wind

ethnic *(ETH-nik)*—related to a group of people and their culture

executive *(ig-ZE-kyuh-tiv)*—the branch of government that makes sure laws are followed

industry *(IN-duh-stree)*—a business which produces a product or provides a service

judicial *(joo-DISH-uhl)*—to do with the branch of government that explains and interprets the laws

legislature *(LEJ-iss-lay-chur)*—a group of elected officials who have the power to make or change laws for a country or state

textile *(TEK-stile)*—a fabric or cloth that has been woven or knitted

tourism *(TOOR-i-zuhm)*—the business of taking care of visitors to a country or place

Read More

Gaines, Ann. *North Carolina.* It's My State! New York: Cavendish Square Publishing, 2014.

Ganeri, Anita. *United States of America: A Benjamin Blog and His Inquisitive Dog Guide.* Country Guides. Chicago: Heinemann Raintree, 2015.

Yasuda, Anita. *What's Great About North Carolina?* Our Great States. Minneapolis: Lerner Publishing Company, 2014.

Internet Sites

FactHound offers a safe, fun way to find Internet sites related to this book. All of the sites on FactHound have been researched by our staff.

Here's all you do:

Visit *www.facthound.com*

Type in this code: 9781515704201

 Check out projects, games and lots more at
www.capstonekids.com

Critical Thinking Using the Common Core

1. Who were the earliest residents of North Carolina? (Key Ideas and Details)

2. According to the timeline on page 18, how old did Andrew Johnson live to be? (Craft and Structure)

3. Congress passed the Civil Rights Act in 1964, making any form of discrimination illegal. What is discrimination? (Craft and Structure)

Index